WE THE PEOPLE

The Santa Fe Trail

by Jean F. Blashfield

Content Adviser: Professor Sherry L. Field,
Department of Social Science Education,
College of Education, The University of Georgia

Reading Adviser: Dr. Linda D. Labbo,
Department of Reading Education,
College of Education, The University of Georgia

✦ COMPASS POINT BOOKS

Minneapolis, Minnesota

Compass Point Books
3722 West 50th Street, #115
Minneapolis, MN 55410

Visit Compass Point Books on the Internet at *www.compasspointbooks.com* or e-mail your request
to *custserv@compasspointbooks.com*

Photographs ©: Archive Photos, cover; Kansas State Historical Society, 4; Corbis, 5; North Wind
Picture Archives, 6; North Wind Picture Archives/Nancy Carter, 7; Unicorn Stock Photos/Ernesto
Burciaga, 9; North Wind Picture Archives, 10, 13; Kansas State Historical Society, 14; North
Wind Picture Archives, 16; Kansas State Historical Society, 17; North Wind Picture Archives, 18;
North Wind Picture Archives/Nancy Carter, 19; Visuals Unlimited, 20; North Wind Picture
Archives, 21; Courtesy Museum of New Mexico/Neg. #7004, 23 top; Kansas State Historical
Society, 23 bottom; Courtesy Museum of New Mexico/Neg. #50505, 24; Kansas State Historical
Society, 25; Courtesy Museum of New Mexico/Neg. #13112/Harold Elderkin, 27; North Wind
Picture Archives, 29, 31, 33; Kansas State Historical Society, 34; Courtesy Museum of New
Mexico/Neg. #15817/Ben Wittick, 36; Courtesy Museum of New Mexico/Neg. #75817/J.R.
Riddle, 38; Courtesy Museum of New Mexico/Neg. #15780/Ben Wittick, 39; North Wind Picture
Archives, 41.

Editors: E. Russell Primm and Emily J. Dolbear
Photo Researcher: Svetlana Zhurkina
Photo Selector: Dawn Friedman
Design: Bradfordesign, Inc.
Cartography: XNR Productions, Inc.

Library of Congress Cataloging-in-Publication Data

Blashfield, Jean F.
   The Santa Fe Trail / by Jean F. Blashfield.
      p. cm. — (We the people)
   Includes bibliographical references and index.
   Summary: Introduces the history and economic purpose of the Santa Fe Trail and the resulting
settlement of the Southwest.
   ISBN 0-7565-0047-8 (lib. bdg.)
   1. Santa Fe Trail—Juvenile literature. [1. Santa Fe Trail. 2. Southwest, New—History.] I. Title.
II. We the people (Compass Point Books).
   F786 .B735 2000
   978—dc21   00-008676

TABLE OF CONTENTS

OPENING UP THE SOUTHWEST

The sharp crack of a bullwhip and the cries of the drivers echoed through the air. Thousands of heavy freight wagons were heading out of Missouri to travel across New Mexico. The head wagon creaked as the oxen strained.

The wagons carried goods to sell in the old city of Santa Fe. During the 1800s, pioneers along

A group of covered wagons travel on the Santa Fe Trail.

A settlement on the Santa Fe Trail

the route were opening up the Southwest of the United States to settlement. The route was called the Santa Fe Trail.

Three hundred years before the opening of the Santa Fe Trail, the Spanish took over Mexico. Their **missionaries,** soldiers, and colonists gradually went farther and farther north from Mexico City. In 1610, they established a capital city called Santa Fe in what would later be called New Mexico.

Spain forced its colonists to trade only with Spain. It wanted all the profits for itself. Dressed

The Adobe Palace in Santa Fe

in leather and shining metal armor, Spanish soldiers arrested traders and others who entered Spanish territory.

Spain also taxed North American goods heavily. In New England, 3 feet (90 centimeters) of **calico** sold for five cents. In Santa Fe, it cost two dollars.

The beautiful San Miguel Chapel still stands in Santa Fe today.

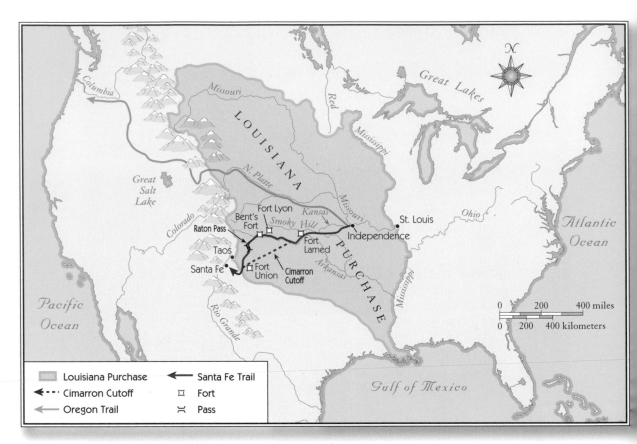

The Santa Fe Trail

The "Father" of the Trail

That kind of profit interested a soldier-turned-trader named William Becknell. In 1821, after almost a decade of fighting, Mexico won its independence from Spain. At the time, Becknell was trading with the Comanche Indians. He rushed from Colorado through the 8,000-foot (2,438-meter) high Raton Pass in the Sangre de Cristo Mountains

The Sangre de Cristo Mountains

9

Travelers make camp near a watering hole on the trail.

into New Mexico. The people of Santa Fe were eager to buy his fabric, pots, combs, and other items.

Hurrying home to Franklin, Missouri, Becknell used his profits to buy huge quantities of luxury items such as fabrics, mirrors, and jewelry.

10

He also bought three wagons and oxen to carry all these goods. With twenty-one strong men to help him, he set out for Santa Fe again.

Becknell didn't think his wagons could make it through the Raton Pass. Instead, he took what came to be called the Cimarron Cutoff, which went through the dry Cimarron Valley of Oklahoma. There was no water source in the valley for three days. Legend says that on Becknell's first trip through the Cimarron Cutoff, his men suffered from thirst until they killed a bison and found water in its stomach. But the challenges of the trip paid off when Becknell sold his goods.

Many businessmen, or **merchants**, soon followed Becknell's trail. In 1824, a group of twenty-five wagons, called a **caravan**, gathered and set off. They carried goods bought in Franklin for $35,000 and sold them in Santa Fe at a profit of $155,000.

A young man who worked as an **apprentice** in a saddle and harness shop in Franklin eagerly watched wagons gather and depart. Christopher Carson, called Kit, hated his work in the shop. He wanted to join the caravan, so he ran away with a wagon train in 1824.

Carson spent his whole life as a frontiers-man, hunter, guide, and army scout. Much of his work was on the Santa Fe Trail. He died on the trail, at Fort Lyon, in 1868, after being thrown from a horse.

Kit Carson stands with his favorite horse, Apache.

After Franklin, the town of Independence became the head of the Santa Fe Trail.

14

THE ROUTE OUT OF MISSOURI

In 1821, Franklin, Missouri, was the town farthest west. It had only a few years of trail glory because floods destroyed it in 1826.

By that time, a new town called Independence was founded. Because Independence was 131 miles (211 kilometers) west of Franklin, the trail was shorter. Independence, Missouri, became the new head of the Santa Fe Trail. The rough-and-tumble town's major job was building and supplying wagons for the Santa Fe Trail, and later for the Oregon Trail.

After leaving Independence, settlers saw nothing but bison and treeless prairie for days. Then, about 120 miles (193 km) from Independence, they reached the town of Council Grove on the Neosho River. It was forested with hardwood trees, and the variety of scenery was welcome.

Loading supplies into wagons for the journey

The stop gave the pioneers a chance to repair

wagon parts and to rest in the shade.

Here also a large oak tree served as an

important trail "post office." People traveling

west left letters in the tree that were picked up and mailed by people traveling east.

Crossing Kansas, the trail went between the Arkansas and Kansas Rivers. At the place where the Arkansas curves to the south, the trail follows the Arkansas River southward. In 1859, the U.S. government set up Fort Larned there. Native Americans often attacked the fort because it was

The trading post in Council Grove

built on their land. Later, they used it as a source of horses and other livestock.

At the point where the Arkansas River turns west again, near Dodge City, travelers had to choose between the Mountain Branch and the Cimarron Cutoff. The Santa Fe Trail along the Mountain Branch was about 900 miles (1,448 km) long. Using the Cimarron Cutoff cut 100 miles (161 km) from the trip.

Fort Larned was a U.S. government fort.

A view of wagon ruts on the Santa Fe Trail, east of the Rockies

THE CUTOFF AND COMANCHE

The history of Comanche attacks against caravans on the Cimarron Cutoff began in 1828. Two traders named McNees and Munroe had ridden ahead of their caravan. They were waiting at a creek when some Native Americans—from which tribe no one knows—shot

A Comanche chief

at them. When the caravan arrived, McNees was dead and Monroe was wounded.

A Comanche warrior on horseback

The next Native Americans the wagoneers saw were the Comanche. The pioneers did not stop to discover whether the Comanche were the ones who had killed McNees. They shot at the Native Americans. The Comanche who escaped warned other Comanche. They kept up their struggle against white men along the Cimarron Cutoff for many years.

Point of Rocks is a rocky cliff along the Cutoff. Here, in 1841, Kit Carson and five other trappers battled about 200 Comanche. The trappers killed their mules and used them for cover. At the end of three days of shooting, the few remaining Comanche abandoned the fight.

THE MOUNTAIN BRANCH

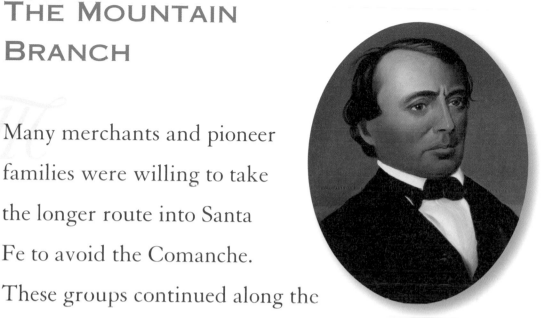

Charles Bent

Many merchants and pioneer families were willing to take the longer route into Santa Fe to avoid the Comanche. These groups continued along the Arkansas River

William Bent

until they reached Bent's Fort. There, the trail turned south through the mountains.

Charles and William Bent were young trappers. In 1829, they sold their furs and bought goods to take on the Santa Fe Trail. In 1833, they built a trading post along the Mountain Branch with a partner named Ceran St. Vrain. Mexican workers built the square **adobe** structure. It had twenty-five rooms around an open court yard. The fort was first known as Fort William and later as Bent's Fort.

Ceran St. Vrain ran a trading post with the Bent brothers.

William Bent was married to a Cheyenne named Owl Woman. Unlike the Comanche, the Cheyenne were friendly and easy to trade with. All Native Americans met peaceably at Bent's Fort, however.

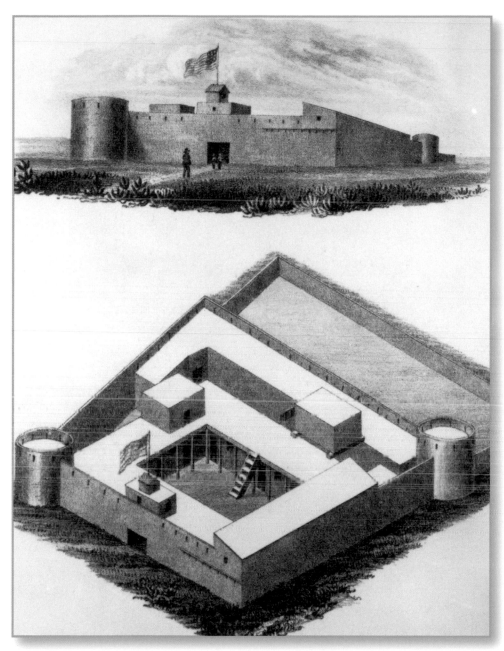

Bent's Fort

In the Mexican War (1846–1848), U.S. troops captured New Mexico in 1846. Charles Bent, who lived in Taos with his Mexican wife, was named governor. When Charles was murdered the following year, his brother, William, grew to hate the fort. He had all the goods and furnishings removed and blew up the huge structure.

Even in ruins, Bent's Fort was an important marker on the way to Raton Pass. For the first forty years of the trail, the area around Bent's Fort was a hair-raising part of the journey. The downward path was so steep that a wagon's wheels had to be locked so that the strongest men could lower it on heavy ropes.

Susan Shelby Magoffin, whose husband was a trader, kept a diary of her 1846 trip. At Raton Pass, she wrote, "It takes a dozen men to steady

"Uncle Dick" Wooton was a famous sheepherder and road builder.

a wagon with all its wheels locked— and for one who is some distance off to hear the crash it makes over the stones is truly alarming."

In 1865, "Uncle Dick" Wooton, a famous sheepherder, sold a huge herd of sheep in California. He used the gold he was paid to blast the steep and dangerous Raton Pass into a smoother road. Everyone except Native Americans had to pay to travel on his road. Later, the Santa Fe Railroad bought the road.

27

INTO SANTA FE

The Mountain Branch and the Cimarron Cutoff came together again in New Mexico about 75 miles (120 km) south of Raton. The U.S. Army built Fort Union there in 1851. From this point, all wagons headed south through the New Mexican towns of Las Vegas and Pecos and into Santa Fe.

The trail ended in the Plaza of Santa Fe in front of the 200-year-old Governor's Palace. All traders who came to Santa Fe had to stop in the plaza so that officials could check and tax their goods. Only then were they free to sell what they had brought.

The Mexican people were especially eager to buy. They wanted glass windows and bottles,

The plaza in Santa Fe

fabrics for new clothing, and small manufactured items such as kitchen tools.

Many traders bought furs and silver goods in New Mexico to sell back east. But the traders never took as many goods back to Missouri as they had brought into New Mexico on the Santa Fe Trail.

29

ON THE TRAIL

One important book about life on the trail, *Commerce of the Prairie*, was published in 1844. Author Josiah Gregg, the son of a Missouri **wheelwright**, was sent west for his health in 1831. His book became a pioneer's guide of what to expect on the trail. Gregg also wisely predicted that if Americans continued to kill bison for "fun," the animal would eventually die out.

Josiah Gregg journeyed over the Santa Fe Trail as a passenger, but most people who traveled the Santa Fe Trail were carrying goods, or **freight**. Unlike the Oregon Trail, a road that brought pioneers to the West, the Santa Fe Trail was mainly a freight highway. The wagons were larger,

Some people worried hunters would wipe out all the bison.

sometimes carrying more than 6,000 pounds (2,725 kilograms). The pioneer wagons of the Oregon Trail carried about 2,000 pounds (900 kg).

The big red-and-blue wagons were pulled by teams of eight oxen or eight mules. In the 1840s, a pair, or **span,** of mules cost about $400 while a pair of oxen could be bought for as little as $20. The men who drove the wagons were called **bullwhackers** or **mule skinners**.

The journey took two to three months. Most traders made only one trip a year, starting in spring. At that time of year, the grass was tall enough for their animals to eat and there was little chance of being caught by winter snows on the return journey. Some tried to squeeze in two trips.

The wagons usually traveled in four straight lines. Then, if they needed protection, they could

Bullwackers drove wagons out on the trail.

Wagon caravans on the trail traveled in lines.

quickly move into a square with the animals inside.
Travelers faced danger from prairie fires, rattle-
snakes, and unexpected blizzards.

Despite the dangers, some women made the trip. They usually traveled with husbands going west to set up businesses. The first-known white family to travel the Santa Fe Trail was the Donohos, in 1833. William Donoho, his wife, Mary, and their nine-month-old daughter went into the hotel business in Santa Fe. However, they later returned to Missouri.

Another woman pioneer on the Santa Fe Trail was Marion Russell. She was only seven in 1852 when she made her first trip along the trail with her mother and brother. She fell in love with the trail and traveled it many times over the years. She met Kit Carson when she was a child in Santa Fe and later married one of Carson's soldiers.

A wagon train arrives in Santa Fe.

DURING THE CIVIL WAR

By 1860, the Santa Fe Trail was the lifeblood of the Southwest. By that year, 3,000 wagons traveled the trail every year. It took 28,000 oxen and 9,000 men to supply the needs of the people at both ends of the trail and along the way.

This fact was not lost on the new Confederate States of America, formed during the Civil War (1861–1865) by the Southern states. In August 1861, Confederate troops captured Fort Fillmore and took New Mexico and Arizona. They wanted their new nation to reach all the way to the Pacific Ocean. The Union soldiers of the North retreated to Fort Union, near where the Mountain Branch and the Cimarron Cutoff joined.

A photograph of La Glorieta Pass from the 1880s

In March 1862, the two sides met again at La Glorieta Pass, in the Sangre de Cristo Mountains near Santa Fe. Union troops destroyed all Confederate supplies, and the Southerners were driven back into Texas. The Battle of La Glorieta Pass ended the Confederacy's only chance to win the Southwest.

The Coming of an End

As the war was going on, the noisy sound of steam engines was already being heard along part of the Santa Fe Trail. The Atchison, Topeka, and Santa Fe—now the Santa Fe Railroad—was being built

An early steam engine in New Mexico

from Kansas to the Southwest. Finally, in 1880, the tracks reached Santa Fe. The days of the wagon trail were over.

In the 1930s, after highways had replaced much of the Santa Fe Trail, ninety-year-old Marion Russell wrote her memories in a book called *Land of Enchantment*. She recalled "the old trail over mountains, through forests, felt the sting of the cold, the oppression of the heat, the drench of rains and the fury of the winds in an old covered wagon." She mused, "My life as I look back seems to have been lived best in those days on the trail."

A wagon crosses the mountains of the Santa Fe Trail.

GLOSSARY

adobe—a brick made of dried earth and straw

apprentice—a person who works for and learns from a skilled tradesperson for a certain amount of time

bullwhackers—people who drive wagons

calico—a cheap cotton fabric

caravan—a group of wagons traveling together

merchants—traders or storekeepers

missionaries—people who travel to new lands to teach a religion

mule skinners—people who drive mules

span—a pair of animals (such as mules)

wheelwright—someone who makes and repairs wheels and wheeled vehicles

DID YOU KNOW?

- Franklin, Missouri, was named after American statesman Benjamin Franklin.

- Pioneers on the Santa Fe Trail often used oxen instead of horses or mules to pull wagons because oxen cost less and stopped to graze less often.

- Cimarron Cutoff was also called Dry Cutoff because of its lack of water.

IMPORTANT DATES

Timeline

1821	Trader William Becknell opens the Santa Fe Trail.
1833	Bent's Fort (first known as Fort William) is built.
1846	The Mexican War begins; U.S. troops capture New Mexico.
1848	The Mexican War ends; the United States gets California, Nevada, Utah, and parts of four other states.
1851	Fort Union is built.
1859	Fort Larned is built.
1879	The Atchison, Topeka and Santa Fe Railroad enters New Mexico.
1880	The railroad reaches Santa Fe, ending a need for the trail.

IMPORTANT PEOPLE

WILLIAM BECKNELL
(1787–1856), *trader*

CHARLES BENT
(1799–1847), *trapper*

WILLIAM BENT
(1809–1869), *trapper*

CHRISTOPHER "KIT" CARSON
(1809–1868), *frontiersman and U.S. Army scout*

JOSIAH GREGG
(1806–1850), *author*

MARION RUSSELL
(1845–1936), *author*

WANT TO KNOW MORE?

At the Library

Bacon, Melvin. *Bent's Fort: Crossroads of Cultures on the Santa Fe Trail.* Brookfield, Conn.: Millbrook Press, 1995.

Lavender, David Sievert. *The Santa Fe Trail.* New York: Holiday House, 1995.

Morris, John Miller. *From Coronado to Escalante: The Explorers of the Spanish Southwest.* New York: Chelsea House Publishers, 1992.

Pelta, Kathy. *The Royal Roads: Spanish Trails in North America.* Austin, Tex : Raintree Steck-Vaughn, 1997.

Wadsworth, Ginger, Ed. *Along the Santa Fe Trail: Marion Russell's Own Story.* Morton Grove, Ill.: Albert Whitman and Co., 1993.

On the Web

Interactive Santa Fe Trail

http://raven.cc.ukans.edu/heritage/research/sft

For a look at the history of the trail and information about the people who traveled it

Santa Fe Trail Center

http://www.larned.net/trailctr/index.htm

For information about the trail's history and useful links

Santa Fe Trail Net

http://www.nmhu.edu/research/sftrail/

For information about historic and contemporary development along the Santa Fe Trail

Through the Mail

City of Independence

Independence Tourism Department

Independence, MO 64050

For information about sites related to the Santa Fe Trail in Independence, Missouri

On the Road

Santa Fe Trail Center

RR 3

Larned, KS 67550

316/285-2054

To visit an indoor and outdoor museum about the Santa Fe Trail.

Or visit the other five National Park Service sites along the trail.

INDEX

About the Author

Jean F. Blashfield has worked for publishers in Chicago, Illinois,
and Washington, D.C. A graduate of the University of Michigan,
she has written about ninety books, most of them for young
people. Jean F. Blashfield has two college-age children and lives
in Delavan, Wisconsin.